Charles Wesley

For All, For All,
My Saviour Died

Herbert Boyd McGonigle

MA, BD, DD, PHD

Former Lecturer at Nazarene Theological College, Dene Road, Didsbury, Manchester, in the classes in Church History, Theology and Wesley Studies, Former Principal of Nazarene Theological College and now Principal Emeritus

British Library Cataloguing in Publication Data.
A catalogue record for this book is available from the British Library

ISBN 978 0 86071 684 6

A Commissioned Publication of

MOORLEYS
Print & Publishing
tel: 0115 932 0643 web: www.moorleys.co.uk

FOREWORD

I am personally indebted to The Revd Harold E Moore who has contributed the Foreword. Harold and Dorothy are members of the Methodist Church and Jeanne and I have known them for more than thirty-four years. On Saturday, March 8, 1986, there was the second Wesley Fellowship gathering in the Nazarene Theological College in Manchester, and Harold brought the Paper, 'The Devotional Use of Charles Wesley Hymns'. *At that time Harold and Dorothy were in charge of South Chadderton Methodist Church, and we came to know them. Many times we have visited Darlington and preached there and it is a joy to know Harold and Dorothy personally. In his book,* Make The Mountains Flow, *given at The Wesley Fellowship at Swanwick, Derbyshire, 2009, he wrote more about Charles Wesley's hymns. Harold knows his subject and he writes enthusiastically of the power and passion of Charles' hymns.*

One of the greatest contributions to my spiritual development and understanding of the Christian gospel has been the hymns of Charles Wesley. Along with scripture, his hymns have been an absorbing and strengthening aid throughout my life. I find that good hymns are an essential part of a Christian's diet, both in private devotions and in public worship. A hymn is a poem or lyric that exalts our God and Heavenly Father. It should be an act of praise, directed to God himself, not simply one of admiration but of adoration. A hymn should enhance our experience of God. It is true that God's grace is wider than the oceans and we are only paddling on the beach. However there is no cause for despair, for God is not completely unknowable. We believe that God is like Jesus and having seen Him, we have seen the Father. A hymn explains what God is like. For example, 'His sovereign grace to all extends.' Sovereign or sovereignty were favourite words with John Calvin but Wesley nevertheless insisted that 'for all, for all, my Saviour died.'

Charles Wesley's hymns derive from his vast knowledge of scripture but also from his contemporary life experience. As this book shows, he met fellow Christians who made God tyrannical and an unjust despot, who had created men and women for hell, without hope of 'holiness and heaven.' Charles Wesley created some eight thousand hymns and the people of the Lord have been singing them with gladness and joy and fervour for two hundred and seventy years. Small wonder that he is called the Church's most celebrated hymn-writer. The book begins and ends by quoting what has been called 'the anthem of militant Arminianism.' What on earth is that some may enquire? When one gets to the final full stop in this book, we will certainly know. I am deeply impressed with this little book. Dr McGonigle's writing is lucid and clear. He draws a fine picture and makes clear the stormy events and relevance of the eighteenth century church. Here is a factual historical exposition but above all it is honest and challenging. So be prepared to be disturbed!

Plenteous he is in truth and grace
He wills that all the fallen race
Should turn, repent, and live
His pardoning grace for all is free
Transgression, sin, iniquity
He freely doth forgive.

Revd Harold E. Moore
Darlington, April 2014

CHARLES WESLEY
For all, for all, my Saviour died

In April 1741 a collection of hymns entitled, *Hymns on God's Everlasting Love,* was published in Bristol by John (1703-1791) and Charles Wesley (1707-1788). Eleven months later, in March 1742, a second collection was published in London under the same title and the two collections added up to forty-four hymns. Unlike the three collections of hymns and sacred poems already published by the Wesley brothers,[1] neither of these collections had any preface, introduction or other explanation, but the sub-title of the Bristol edition made its purpose plain: '*To which is added, The Cry of a Reprobate and The Horrible Decree.*' The first hymn in this collection sets the tone for what was to follow. It began:

Father, whose *everlasting love*
Thy only Son for sinners gave
Whose grace to *all* did *freely* move
And sent Him down *a world to save.*[2]

Even before the theological intention of the hymn is grasped, the repeated use of italics in the seventeen stanzas point the way. Words and phrases like *everlasting love, all, freely, a world to save, who died for all, general Saviour of mankind, undistinguishing regard,* and, *sufficient, sovereign, saving* grace, indicate the polemical intention of the publication. If there were any people in England in 1741 who knew about John

---

[1] *Hymns and Sacred Poems*, Published by John Wesley and Charles Wesley, London, (1739). *Hymns and Sacred Poems,* Published by John Wesley and Charles Wesley, London, (1740). *A Collection of Psalms and Hymns,* Published by John Wesley, (1741), London.
[2] Charles Wesley, *The Poetical Works*, Vol. 3, p. 3.

and Charles Wesley only from the latter's hymns, this collection would have come as something of a shock. The three collections of hymns already published, comprising almost four hundred pieces, contained some of the hymns that were among the most popular that Charles wrote, and which are still sung today. They included, *And can it be?*, *Arise, my soul, arise*, *Christ from whom all blessings flow*, *Come O Thou traveller unknown*, *Depth of mercy, can there be?*, *God of all power, and truth, and grace*, *O for a thousand tongues to sing*, *O love Divine, what hast Thou done?* and, *O for a heart to praise my God.*' Nowhere in these three collections is there any hint of theological controversy. Charles Wesley had already made clear his stand on the question – for whom did Christ die? He gave his answer in 1740, in his ever-popular, *A Hymn for the Anniversary Day of One's Conversion*, commonly known from its seventh stanza, *'O for a thousand tongues to sing.'*

See all your sins on Jesus laid
The Lamb of God was slain
His soul was once an offering made
For *every soul* of man.[3]

What was new in these *Hymns on God's Everlasting Love* was not the emphasis on the universal reach both of God's love and the benefits of Christ's atonement; rather it was their open war on any attempt to limit universal love and universal saving grace. The opening hymn, *Father, whose everlasting love*, had the following stanzas:

For those who at the judgment day
On Him they pierced shall *look* with pain
The Lamb for every castaway
For *every soul of man* was slain.

---

3   Charles Wesley, *The Poetical Works*, Vol. 2, p. 301.

Thou hast compelled the lost to die
Hast *reprobated* from Thy face
Hast others saved, but them *passed by*
Or mocked with only *damning grace.*

Still shall the hellish doctrine stand
And Thee for its dire author claim?
No! let it sink at Thy command
Down to the pit from whence it came.

Arise, O God, maintain Thy cause
The fullness of the *Gentiles* call
Lift up the standard of thy Cross
And *all* shall own Thou diedst for all.[4]

Another hymn in this collection gloried in the universal love and grace of God and it didn't require any marginal citations or footnotes to indicate the doctrines it repudiated.

For me, *for* me, *the Saviour died*
Surely Thy grace for all is free
I *feel* it now by faith *applied*
Who died for all hath died for me.

No dire decree obtained Thy seal
Or fixed the unalterable doom
Consigned my unborn soul to hell
Or damned me from my mother's womb.

Loving to every *man Thou art*
Sinners, ye all His grace may prove
He bears you all upon His heart
God is not *hate*, but God is *love.*[5]

---

4   Charles Wesley, *The Poetical Works*, Vol. 3, pp. 4, 5.
5   Charles Wesley, *The Poetical Works*, Vol. 3, p. 33.

If anyone thought that Charles Wesley was merely interested in debating a theological point, two final verses from another hymn in the collection dispelled any illusion that these hymns were just an academic exercise in speculative theology.

My life I here present
My heart's last drop of blood
O let it all be freely spent
In proof that Thou art good.
Art good to all that breathe
Who all may pardon have
Thou willest not the sinner's death
But all the world *wouldst* save.

O take me at my word
But arm me with Thy power
Then call me forth to suffer, Lord
To meet the fiery hour.
In death will I proclaim
That all *may* hear Thy call
And clap my hands amidst the flame
And shout – HE DIED FOR ALL.[6]

What was all this poetic vehemence about? For what was Charles Wesley prepared to be a martyr? The answer lies in what happened in Bristol three years earlier, in April 1739. John Wesley had come to Bristol at the invitation of George Whitefield. He found to his astonishment and deep chagrin that his colleague was preaching in the fields and open spaces around Bristol. Then came the second shock. Whitefield announced that he was leaving the following week for Georgia and that he was sure John Wesley was the man sent by God to

---

[6] Charles Wesley, *The Poetical Works,* Vol. 3, pp. 37, 38.

carry on the 'Methodist' work in the city. So on Monday April 2, 1739, at 4 in the afternoon, John Wesley preached for the first time out of doors. In the following weeks he was engaged in this 'field preaching' two or three times every day and giving pastoral oversight to the Bristol Methodists.

The work was progressing rapidly until an anonymous letter began to circulate in Bristol. John was surprised at the tone of the letter and he hesitated on how he ought to answer. In a letter to James Hutton, dated Bristol, April 30, 1739, he spoke of the letter.

> I was in much doubt how to proceed. Our dear brethren, before I left London, and our brother Whitefield, and our brother Chapman since, had conjured me to enter into no disputes, least of all concerning predestination, because this people was so deeply prejudiced for it. The same was my own inclination. But this evening I received a long letter (almost a month after date) charging me roundly with 'resisting and perverting the truth as it is in Jesus' by preaching against God's decree of predestination. I had not done so yet, but I questioned whether I ought not now to declare the whole counsel of God. Especially since that letter had been long handed about in Bristol before it was sealed and brought to me, together with another, wherein also the writer exhorts his friends to avoid me as a false teacher. However, I thought it best to walk gently, and so said nothing this day.[7]

In his *Diaries* John Wesley speaks about what happened at Bristol. On Wednesday April 25, he says, 'Writ upon predestination.' On Thursday April 26, he commented: 'Writ to Fetter Lane … Appealed to God concerning predestination.' On Saturday April 28: 'Sermon upon predestination.' Then comes the sermon. Sunday April 29: 'Bowling Green, "Free Grace," four thousand there ….Monday April 30 ….Brick-yard, "Free Grace," two struck, one comforted!' There is no more mention

---

[7]   John Wesley, *Works [BE]*, Vol. 25, p. 639.

of the sermon 'Free Grace' in either John Wesley's *Diaries* or *Journal*. Years earlier he had studied the question carefully as he wrestled with Article 17 of the *Thirty-Nine Articles* in preparation for ordination in 1725. His views on election and predestination were certainly fixed long before he came to Bristol but these doctrines had not had any mention in his preaching.

The outcome was that in order to settle rumours and speculation John Wesley determined to preach openly on the subject. If he thought this would put an end to the disputing, he was sadly mistaken. The sermon he preached on Sunday 29 April 1739 at the Bowling Green in Bristol would lead eventually to the 'Methodists' dividing into two theological camps - Wesleyan Methodists and Calvinistic Methodists. The sermon, *Free Grace*, was based on Romans 8:32. 'He who did not spare His own Son but gave him up for us all...'[8] The sermon made two main points; God's grace is free in all and free for all. It was the second point that was in contention for while John Wesley stressed that God's saving grace was free for all, other 'Methodists' were stressing that saving grace is offered only to the elect. The controversy that first appeared in Christian theology with Augustine in the fifth century, and had rumbled on through the Continental and English Reformations, and in particular with England's 17th century Puritans, now surfaced among the Bristol Methodists. What was at stake was the extent of saving grace, or stated soteriological, for whom did Christ die? - for the sins of the whole world or only for those of the elect?

---

[8] John Wesley, *Works [BE]*, Vol. 3, pp. 542-563. Although 'Free Grace' was important in Bristol, there is no report that it was preached ever again. Perhaps John Wesley thought that it was best laid aside and never referred to.

The controversy brought to light a particular phrase from John Calvin's *Theological Institutes* that would become a kind of theological football in the coming years. In Book 3 of the *Institutes* Calvin had written:

> I again ask how it is that the fall of Adam involves so many nations, with their infant children, in eternal death without remedy, unless that it so seemed meet to God? Here the most loquacious tongues must be dumb. The decree, I admit, is dreadful, and yet it is impossible to deny that God foreknew what the end of man was to be before He made him, and foreknew, because He had so ordained by His decree. Should any one here inveigh against the prescience of God, he does so rashly and unadvisedly. For why, pray, should it be made a charge against the heavenly Judge, that he was not ignorant of what was to happen? .... Nor ought it is to seem absurd when I say, that God not only foresaw the fall of the first man, and in him the ruin of his posterity, but also at his own pleasure arranged it. For as it belongs to his wisdom to foreknow all future events, so it belongs to his power to rule and govern them by his hand.[9]

Calvin's words, *decretum quidem horrible fateor*, have been variously translated as 'the decree is terrible' 'awful' or 'dreadful.' In the context of the whole argument, Calvin's Latin is probably best translated as, 'The decree, I admit, is awesome,' but the word 'horrible' was seized upon and so the phrase, 'the horrible decree' gained currency. In his *Free Grace* sermon John Wesley repudiated the theology of absolute predestination.

> Call it therefore by whatever name you please – election, preterition, predestination, or reprobation, it comes in the end to

---

[9]   John Calvin, *The Institutes of the Christian Religion*, (Edinburgh, 1962), translated by Henry Beveridge, Vol. 11, p. 232. In what is generally agreed to be the definitive translation of the *Institutes*, F. L. Battles has: 'The decree is dreadful indeed, I confess.' In a footnote J. T. McNeill added: 'Calvin is awestruck but unrelenting in his declaration that God is the author of reprobation.' *Library of Christian Classics*, Vol. XXI, p. 955.

the same thing. The sense of all is plainly this: By virtue of an eternal, unchangeable, irresistible decree of God, one part of mankind are infallibly saved, and the rest infallibly damned... This is the blasphemy contained in the 'horrible decree' of predestination... Sing, O hell, and rejoice ye that are under the earth! For God, even the mighty God, hath spoken, and devoted to death thousands of souls, from the rising up of the sun unto the going down thereof. Here, O death, is thy sting. They shall not, cannot escape, for the mouth of the Lord hath spoken.... Nations yet unborn, or ever they have done good or evil, are doomed never to see the light of life, but thou shalt gnaw upon them for ever and ever. This is the blasphemy contained in 'the horrible decree' of predestination. And here I fix my foot. On this I join issue with every assertor of it.... You say you will 'prove it by the Scripture.' Hold! What will you prove by Scripture? That God is worse than the devil! It cannot be. Whatever the Scriptures proves, it never can prove this.... No Scriptures can mean that God is not love, or that his mercy is not over all his works. That is, whatever it prove beside, no scripture can prove predestination.[10]

John Wesley published his *Free Grace* sermon and soon after it evoked a reply from George Whitefield, entitled, *A Letter to the Rev. Mr John Wesley*.[11] Both publications added fuel to the fire and this was the theological fracas that Charles Wesley found when he arrived in Bristol for the first time in August 1739. He threw himself into the work of preaching and visiting and quite soon we read references in his *Letters* and *Journal* to disputes about predestination. It was first reported that Charles was 'a strong Predestinarian' so he decided to put the matter straight in his next sermon.

> We called at Mr Cottle's and heard the people were very much exasperated against me, it being everywhere reported that I am a strong predestinarian. Much pains had been taken to represent

[10] John Wesley, *Works [BE]*, Vol. 3, pp. 547-556.
[11] The full text is in A. Dallimore, *George Whitefield*, Vol. 2, pp. 551-569.

me as such. We judged this a call for me to *declare* myself, if the weavers, who were to rise, would suffer me. We found about two thousand waiting. I let my brother pray, and then began abruptly. 'If God be for us, who can be against us? He that spared not his own son but delivered him up for us all, how shall he not with him, also freely give us all things?' [Rom. 8: 31-32]. God opened my mouth so as seldom before. I felt what I spoke, while offering Christ to all; in much love I besought the Dissenters not to lose their charity for me because I was of opinion God would have *all* men to be saved. For an hour and a half, I strongly called all sinners to the Saviour of the world. My strength do I ascribe unto Him. No one opened his mouth against me. The devil fled before us, and I believe he will no more slander me with being a predestinarian.[12]

Charles remained in Bristol almost until the end of 1739 and then returned to London. He spent most of the following year supporting John in the growing problems with the Moravians and made one preaching visit to Bristol. In April 1741 he returned to Bristol and this coincided with the publication of his *Hymns on God's Everlasting Love*. For some time John Cennick, the Bristol school-master and formerly a strong supporter of both the Wesleys, had been emerging as the leader of a group of Bristol Methodists and was strongly opposed to the Wesleys' teaching both on universal grace and Christian perfection. The *Hymns* were published while the dispute was still simmering. In a letter to Whitefield, Cennick complained about Charles' stand against predestination.

That you might come quickly, I have written a second time. I sit solitary, like Eli, waiting what will become of the ark. My trouble increases daily. How glorious did the gospel seem once to flourish in Kingswood. I spake of the everlasting love of Christ with sweet power, but now brother Charles is suffered to

---

[12] Charles Wesley, *The Manuscript Journal of The Reverend Charles Wesley*, Vol 1, p. 213.

open his mouth against this truth, while the frightened sheep gaze and fly, as if no shepherd was among them. Brother Charles pleases the world with universal redemption, and brother John follows him in everything. No atheist can preach more against predestination than they, and all who believe election are counted enemies of God, and called so. Fly, dear brother, I am in the midst of the plague.[13]

More information on the doctrinal foment at Bristol is found in John Wesley's *Diary* and *Journal*. In March 1741 he published a twenty-six page pamphlet entitled, *Serious Considerations on Absolute Predestination: Extracted from a Late Author*.[14] The 'late author' was the Quaker apologist, Robert Barclay, and Wesley used the Bristol publisher, Robert Farley, who also published the hymns. Three months later John followed this up with another publication, *A Dialogue between a Predestinarian and his Friend*.[15] Six months later appeared yet another pamphlet, *The Scripture Doctrine Concerning Predestination, Election, and Reprobation. Extracted from a late Author, by John Wesley*.[16] The 'late author' was the 17th century Baptist writer, Henry Haggar.

Whether or not John Cennick was correct in saying that John Wesley followed his brother Charles in everything, there is no doubt that on the question of the extent of saving grace, the two brothers were of one mind. Recent research has shown that John and Charles increasingly differed in their convictions on a number of issues, but on the question of predestination they spoke and wrote as one. The Wesleys well knew that Scripture speaks about election and predestination and they repeatedly

---

13 Luke Tyerman, *Life and Times of the Rev. John Wesley*, (1870), Vol. 1, p. 344.
14 John Wesley, *Works [BE]*, Vol. 26, p. 55.
15 John Wesley, *Journal*, Vol. 2, p. 473.
16 John Wesley, *Journal*, Vol. 2, p. 473.

made clear that their opposition was targeted, not at these concepts as such, but against what they believed were <u>absolute</u> interpretations of predestination that necessarily entailed a doctrine of reprobation. John went as far as to concede that if anyone could demonstrate a doctrine of predestination that did not involve a doctrine of reprobation he would embrace it.[17] In Charles's hymns written against 'the horrible decree,' the target <u>is always reprobation</u>.

John Wesley defined his own and his brother's understanding of predestination, in his enlarged version of Haggar's tract.

> The Scriptures tell us plainly what predestination is: it is God's fore-appointing obedient believers to salvation, not without, but according to, his foreknowledge of all their works, from the foundation of the world. And so likewise he predestinates or fore-appoints, all disobedient unbelievers to damnation, not without, but according to, his foreknowledge of all their works from the foundation of the world. We may consider this a little farther. God from the foundation of the world foreknew all men's believing or not believing: and according to this his foreknowledge, he chose or elected all obedient believers, as such, to salvation; and refused or reprobated all disobedient unbelievers to damnation. Thus the Scriptures teach us to consider election and reprobation 'according to the foreknowledge of God, from the foundation of the world.'[18]

In his hymns Charles Wesley spelled out this understanding of predestination based on God's foreknowledge and also made constant reference to another doctrinal point that John emphasised in all his anti-predestination publications. This was the deduction he drew from the doctrine that Christ died only for the sins of the elect. God, in justice, could not condemn the non-elect for unbelief, or for continued impenitence, or because

---

[17]   John Wesley, *Works*, Vol. 10, p. 211.
[18]   John Wesley, *A Preservative Against Unsettled Notions in Religion*, London, 1839.

11

they refused the good news the gospel brings – because, on the ultra-Calvinist scheme of salvation, there was no gospel for the non-elect. God did not love them, Christ did not die for them, and the Holy Spirit did not work effectively in their hearts. It was this *reductio absurdum*, as he saw it, that Charles attacked so relentlessly.

The righteous God consigned
Them over to their doom
And sent the Saviour of mankind
To damn them from the womb.
To damn for falling short
Of what they could not do
For not believing the report
Of that which was not true.[19]

Although Charles Wesley thought highly of Whitefield, he was irritable that so much of Whitefield's doctrines were spreading among the Methodist in Bristol.

> By the time this reaches Bristol, I suppose you will be in London. George Whitefield, you know, is come. His fair words are not to be trusted to; for his actions show most unfriendly.... George Whitefield came into the desk while I was showing the believers privilege, i.e. power over sin. After speaking some time I desired him to preach. He did – predestination, perseverance, and the necessity of sinning. Afterwards I mildly expostulated with him, asking if he would commend me for preaching the opposite doctrines in his orphan-house; protesting against the publishing his answer to you, and labouring for peace to the utmost of my power. Asked whether he held reprobation, which he avowed, so also his intention of preaching it upon the housetop. Behold, the hope of him is in vain. He is determined to follow his friend Seward, with equal steps.[20]

---

[19] Charles Wesley, *The Poetical Works*, Vol. 3, pp. 35, 36.
[20] Charles Wesley, *Works [BE]*, Vol. 26, p. 54.

It was inevitable that this dispute among the Bristol Methodists would result in strained relations between former friends and so it proved. John Cennick and a group of his supporters left the Wesleys and began meeting separately. Although Charles Wesley's friendship with George Whitefield would survive all the conflicts, yet he was deeply unhappy with Whitefield's support for predestination.

> One, who in fear of God, and mistrust of himself, had heard Mr Whitefield, assured me he had preached barefaced reprobation. The people fled before the reprobating lion. But again and again, as he observed them depart, the preacher of sad tidings called them back, with general offers of salvation. Vain and empty offers indeed! What availed his telling them that, for aught he knew, they might be all elect. He did not believe them all elect; he could not, therefore he only mocked them with an empty word of invitation, and if God sent him to preach the gospel to every creature, God, according to his scheme, sent him to deceive the greatest part of mankind.[21]

This entry in Charles' *Journal* barely conceals his ire at Whitefield's doctrines of predestination and reprobation, and a letter written soon after to his brother John makes no attempt to conceal his indignation.

> I am exceedingly afraid lest predestination should be propagated among us in a more subtle and dangerous manner than has hitherto been attempted. Mr Whitefield preached holiness very strongly and 'free grace' to all; yet at the same time, he uses expressions which necessarily imply reprobation. He wraps it up in smoother language than before, in order to convey the poison more successfully. Our Society, on this account, go to hear him without any scruple or dread. We have sufficiently seen the fatal effects of this devilish doctrine already, so that we cannot keep at too great a distance from it. For my part, by the grace of God, I

---

[21] Charles Wesley, *The Manuscript Journal of The Reverend Charles Wesley*, Vol. 1, p. 303.

never will be reconciled to reprobation, nor join with those who hold it.[22]

Charles Wesley took great care for all them that came for salvation and was careful to show them the Lord's way of repentance and faith. Between his first and second visit to Bristol, he spent his days preaching, teaching and ministering, especially to those nearing death. Wesley felt drawn to sister Hooper, an old saint and ready to join the triumphant host. For a week he kept up his visits and it is remarkable what he wrote in his *Journal*.

> Found our sister Hooper sick of love. Her body too, sunk under it.... Passed an hour in weeping with some that wept, then rejoiced over our sister Hooper.... Saw my dear friend again in great bodily weakness, but strong in the Lord, and in the power of his might... I spoke with her physician, who said he had little hope of her recovery. "Only she has no dread upon her spirits, which is generally the worst symptom. Most people die for fear of dying, but I never met with those people as yours. They are, none of them, afraid of death, but calm, and patient, and resigned to the last".... Found our sister Hooper just at the haven. She expressed, while able to speak, her fullness of confidence and love, her desire to be with Christ, her grief at the preaching the other gospel. Some of her words were, "Does Mr Cennick still preach his wretched doctrine?".... At my last visit I saw her in her latest conflict. The angel of death was coming and but a few moments between her and blessed eternity. We poured out our souls to God for her, her children, ourselves, the church and ministers, and all mankind.... We knelt down and gave God thanks from the ground of our heart.[23]

The on-going predestinarian dispute in Bristol not only brought John Cennick and George Whitefield into controversy with

---

[22]   Charles Wesley, *Works [BE]*, Vol. 26, p. 65.
[23]   Charles Wesley, *The Manuscript Journal of the Reverend Charles Wesley*, Vol. 1, pp. 302-304.

Charles Wesley, but also involved Howell Harris, the Welsh 'Methodist.' Harris eventually emerged as a kind of peace-maker between the Wesleyan and Calvinistic Methodists. Charles was delighted to meet Howell but as time passed he noticed that Howell made friends with the Calvinists rather than with the Arminianists. On Tuesday November 4, 1740, Charles wrote in his *Journal*.

> At Kingswood Mr Cennick showed me a letter from Howell Harris, wherein he justified poor Mr Seward, and talked of declaring against us himself. With the loss of him and all things, I am commanded to preach the gospel to every creature. I did so to the colliers, from Titus 2:11, and was carried out more than ever before, till all were drowned in tears of love. While I was testifying Christ died for all, Mr Cennick, in the hearing of many, gave me the lie. I calmly told him afterwards, "If I speak not the truth as it is in Jesus, may I decrease and you increase."[24]

A week later Charles felt led to invite Howell Harris again to further their conversation.

> Sent a messenger to Howell Harris, with the following letter: My dearest friend and brother. In the name of Jesus Christ I beseech you, if you have his glory and the good of souls at heart, come immediately, and meet me here. I trust we shall never be two in time or eternity. O my brother, I am grieved that Satan should get a moment's advantage over us, and am ready to lay my neck under your feet for Christ's sake. If your heart is as my heart, hasten, in the name of our dear Lord, to your second self.[25]

Two weeks later Charles wrote in his *Journal*.

> Gave the Sacrament to our sister Taylor, dying in triumph. Here is another witness to the truth of the gospel. Commend me to a religion upon which I can trust my soul, while entering into

---

[24] Charles Wesley, *The Manuscript Journal of the Reverend Charles Wesley*, Vol. 1, p. 284.

[25] Charles Wesley, *The Manuscript Journal of the Reverend Charles Wesley*, Vol. 1, p. 286.

eternity. Expounded the lesson at Kingswood. It was 6th of Hebrews. I prayed Christ our Teacher to enlighten the people with me, and began my discourse with fear and trembling. The Spirit gave me utterance. I calmly warned them against apostasy, and spake with great tenderness and caution. But who can stand before envy and bigotry? The strong ones were offended. The poison of Calvin has drunk up their spirit of love. Anne Ayling and Anne Davis could not refrain from railing. John Cennick never offered to stop them. Alas! We have set the wolf to keep the sheep! God gave me great moderation toward him, who, for many months, has been undermining our doctrine and authority.[26]

Seven months later Harris asked Wesley if he might attend their services and Charles invited him.

I bade him come in God's name. We were singing,
Thee triumphantly we praise
Vie with all thy hosts above
Shout thine universal grace
Thine everlasting love.

when William Hooper, by my order, brought him. I prayed according to God, gave out a hymn which we might all join in. The hand of the Lord was upon me. I asked Howell whether he had a mind to speak, and sat by for half an hour, while he gave an account of his conversion by *irresistible grace*, mixing with his experience the impossibility of falling, God's unchangeableness, &. I could not but observe the ungenerousness of my friend, and after hearing him long and patiently, was moved to rise up and ask in the name of Jesus, 'Ye that are spiritual, doth the Spirit which is in you suffer me still to keep silence, and let my brother go on? Can I do it without bringing the blood of these souls upon me?' A woman first cried out, 'The wounds of Jesus answer No.' Then many others repeated, No, no, no,' and a whole cloud of witnesses

[26] Charles Wesley, *The Manuscript Journal of the Reverend Charles Wesley*, Vol. 1, p. 292.

arose, declaring, 'Christ died for all.' I asked again, Would you have my brother Harris proceed, or would you not? If you would hear him, I will be silent all night. Again they forbade me in strong words upon which I gave out,

Break forth into joy
Your Comforter sing,

They did break forth as the sounds of many waters or mighty thunderings. O what a burst of joy was there in the midst of us! The God and Saviour of all men was provoked and magnified his universal love.[27]

Charles doesn't tell us if they went on to sing the following stanza but he had clearly not chosen a hymn at random to drown Harris' testimony.

For Jesus the Lord hath comforted man
The sinner restored, Nor suffered in vain
To bring us to heaven, when raised from our fall
His life He hath given a ransom for all.[28]

This summary account of the predestination dispute among the Bristol Methodists, particularly in 1741, is necessary in order to understand why John and Charles Wesley published their two volumes, *Hymns on God's Everlasting Love*. Although both the brothers' names were on the title pages, there is no question that all forty-four hymns came from the pen of Charles Wesley. The hymns were Charles' contribution to the theological contention that had evoked John's *Free Grace* sermon and his tracts against rigid predestination. There was much more passion and fervour, and indeed indignation, in Charles's

---

[27] Charles Wesley, *The Manuscript Journal of the Reverend Charles Wesley*, Vol. 1, p. 316.
[28] Charles Wesley, *The Poetical Works*, Vol. 2, p. 170.

hymns against predestination than in John's pages. There is a kind of poetic savagery in Charles' denunciation of what he pilloried as 'the horrible decree.'

Still shall the hellish doctrine stand
And Thee for its dire author claim?
No: let it sink at Thy command
Down to the pit from whence it came.

Arise, O God, maintain Thy cause
The fullness of the *Gentiles* call
Lift up the standard of Thy cross
And *all* shall own Thou diedst for all.[29]

Until John Wesley began his field-preaching in Bristol in April 1739, there is almost a complete absence of any mention of debates about election and predestination in the publication of either of the Wesley brothers. There is, however, indisputable evidence that John and Charles, reared in the Epworth rectory, were brought up in a household that gave short shrift to any form of Calvinistic predestination. Their father, Samuel Wesley, answered questions for many years in the *Athenian Gazette*, a two-page, twice weekly folio edited by his brother-in-law, John Dunton. Samuel's answers to questions about predestination reveal his bias against absolute predestination and corollary doctrines. Later, when John Wesley was preparing to take holy orders in 1725, he asked his mother's advice on how to understand Article XVII of the *Thirty-Nine Articles*. Susanna replied.

> The doctrine of predestination, as maintained by the rigid
> Calvinists, is very shocking, and ought utterly to be abhorred;
> because it directly charges the most holy God with being the
> author of sin. 'Tis certainly inconsistent with the justice and

---

goodness of God to lay any man under either a physical or moral necessity of committing sin, and then punish him for doing it. I do firmly believe that God from eternity hath elected some to everlasting life. But then I humbly conceive that this election is founded on his foreknowledge, according to that in the 8th of Romans. …Whom in his eternal prescience God saw would make a right use of their powers, and accept of offered mercy…. He did predestinate, adopt for his children, his peculiar treasure. And that they might be conformed to the image of his Son, he called them to himself, by his external Word, the preaching of the gospel, and internally by his Holy Spirit…. This is the sum of what I believe concerning predestination, which I think is agreeable to the analogy of faith, since it never derogates from God's free grace, nor impairs the liberty of man.[30]

Susanna added that if these thoughts did not satisfy John, then he should consult his father Samuel. Although in another context Susanna confessed, 'Tis an unhappiness almost peculiar to our family that your father and I seldom think alike,'[31] clearly the Epworth rector and his wife did think alike on questions of election and predestination. It was in this doctrinal atmosphere of anti-Calvinistic theology that John and Charles Wesley were nurtured and all the evidence points to their imbibing what might be called Epworth Arminianism. Samuel Wesley did not label his theology Arminian, nor did John and Charles, at least in the early decades of the Revival. While that reference to the teachings of the Dutch theologian, James Arminius, would have been theologically accurate, there were two main reasons for the Wesleys' hesitancy to subscribe to Arminianism. First, the theology they espoused owed almost nothing directly to Arminius, while owing almost everything to the overt anti-predestinarianism of 17th century high church Anglican theologians like Jeremy Taylor, Henry Hammond,

---

[30] John Wesley, *Works [BE]*, Vol. 25, pp. 179, 180.
[31] *Manuscript Letter*, Wesley's Chapel, City Road, E.C.1.

Peter Heylyn and George Bull. Secondly, both Samuel and his sons were only too well aware that in the first half of the 18th century, much of English Arminianism had descended into a kind of Latitudinarian humanism, often characterised by a reductionist Christology, a reluctance to emphasise Trinitarianism and, in some particular instances, an open aversion to the doctrine of original sin.

As the predestinarian conflict among the Methodists developed into the 1750s, 60s and 70s, John and Charles Wesley overcame their reluctance to adopt the description Arminian and John launched the *Arminian Magazine* in 1778. He explained the express intentions of the new publication. I hang out no false colours. 'Scriptural,' 'Christian,' etc. are all equivocal words. I mean a magazine purposely wrote to defend Universal Redemption.'[32] Although the proposal to launch the *Arminian Magazine* was John Wesley's personal initiative, it had Charles' full support. A few years earlier Lady Selina had written a circular letter inviting evangelical clergymen to attend John Wesley's preachers' Conference in Bristol and stage a demonstration in protest against his 'papist' views. She enclosed a personal letter to Charles Wesley, whose close friendship with the Countess was well known. The letter was intended to drive a wedge between the two brothers.

> I shall ever, from Scripture, as well as the happy demonstration of truth to my own conscience, maintain the sufficiency of that glorious sacrifice for sinners as the *whole* of my salvation, abhorring all merit in man, and giving that glory to Jesus Christ, which alone to Him eternally belongs. You must see in this view, that neither partiality nor prejudice has anything to do in this whole affair. Principles that make shipwreck of faith, and of course of a good conscience, are what I object to; and no gloss, ever so finely drawn over these apostate sentiments, can alter their nature or

---

[32] John Wesley, *Letters*, 6:284.

consequence to me....As you have no part in this matter, I find it difficult to blame your brother to you; while as an honest man I must pity and not less regard you, as you must suffer equal disgrace, and universal distrust, from the supposed union with him. I know you so well, and believe the Lord who brings light with truth, will also show you, that no mean disguises, or a less interesting point, could thus influence me in that stand I make.[33]

If Lady Huntingdon had thought that Charles Wesley was in any way less opposed to a Calvinistic interpretation of predestination than his brother John, she was very much mistaken. Her letter, intended to alienate Charles from his brother, had the opposite effect. On the back of the letter Charles wrote, 'Lady Huntingdon's last. Unanswered by John Wesley's brother.'[34] In a letter to John he pointedly wrote, 'I have just finished Brandt's 'History of the Synod of Dort.' Cannot you oblige us with a short extract out of him?, out of 'Redemption Redeemed' or whom you choose? I verily think you are *called* to drive reprobation back to its own place.'[35] The references here to Charles Wesley's reading are very interesting. What he short-hands as 'Brandt's History of the Synod of Dort' refers to the large and exhaustive four-volume history, *The Reformation and other Ecclesiastical Transactions in and about the Low Countries ...down to the Famous Synod of Dort.* This was the work of the Remonstrant scholar Gerard Brandt. Charles' reference to 'Redemption Redeemed' indicates that he knew John Goodwin's 1651 work, *Redemption Redeemed of the World by Jesus Christ, is by Expressness of Scripture, clearness of Argument, countenance of the best authority, as well Ancient as Modern, Vindicated and Asserted in the Just Latitude and Extent of it.* Although John did not

---

[33] Thomas Jackson, *The Life of the Rev. Charles Wesley*, (1841), Vol. 11, pp. 255, 256.

[34] Thomas Jackson, *The Life of the Rev. Charles Wesley*, (1841), Vol. 2, p. 257.

[35] Thomas Jackson, *The Life of the Rev. Charles Wesley*, (1841), Vol. 2, p. 257.

respond immediately to Charles' request to publish an extract from Brandt's history, he did include an extract in the first issue of the *Arminian Magazine*.

When all the relevant material is gathered about Charles Wesley's reading, particularly concerning the doctrines of grace, there is clear evidence to designate him as a high Anglican Arminian. His protests against what he saw as extreme predestination teaching were as emphatic as anything that came from the pen of his brother John and frequently more impassioned and more polemical. His methodology in *Hymns on God's Everlasting Love* was to impersonate particular people and expose the doctrine he was refuting with biting irony. Charles impersonates a sincere seeker after God who has heard the good news of universal grace.

O *Saviour of all* in *Adam* that fell
Attend to our call, and set to Thy seal
Our thankful rehearsal if Thou dost approve
Of grace universal, and infinite love.

If *all* men were *dead*, and fell in the fall
Our *Adam,* our Head, the type of us all
Our *Adam* from heaven the loss dost retrieve
For all Thou wast given, that all might believe.

In *Adam* we died, in Thee we *may* live
Thy merits applied we all *may* receive
The common salvation to all doth belong
To every nation, and people, and tongue.[36]

---

[36] Charles Wesley, *The Poetical Works*, Vol. 3, pp. 7, 8.

In the hymn entitled, 'The Horrible Decree,' Charles Wesley impersonates the preacher who denies universal grace.
Oh Horrible Decree
Worthy of whence it came
Forgive their hellish blasphemy
Who charge it on the Lamb.
Whose pity Him inclined
To leave His throne above
The friend and Saviour of mankind
The God of grace and love.[37]

Charles then pillories what he calls 'the other gospel,' meaning the predestination creed.
Sinners, abhor the fiend
His other *gospel* hear
The God of truth did not intend
The things His word declare;
He offers grace to all
Which most cannot embrace
Mocked with an ineffectual call
And insufficient grace.

The righteous God consigned
Them over to their doom
And sent the Saviour of mankind
To damn them from the womb;
To damn for falling short
Of what they could not do
For not believing the report
Of that which was not true.

---

[37] Charles Wesley, *The Poetical Works*, Vol. 3, p. 34.

He did not them bereave
Of life, or stop their breath
His grace He only would not give
And starved their souls to death.
Satanic sophistry!
But still, all gracious God
They charge the sinner's death on Thee
Who bought them with Thy blood.[38]

No one reading these *Hymns on God's Everlasting Love* could doubt the ferocity of Charles Wesley's repugnance of any attempt to limit what the title declared – God's universal and everlasting love. Whatever particular point of the predestination creed Charles may be attacking in any particular hymn, this is always his intended target. He simply <u>cannot</u> believe that God did not love the whole world of men and women created in His image – a whole world of men and women for whom Christ died an atoning death – and a whole world of men and women who *may* be saved if they repent and believe the gospel.

Although John and Charles Wesley entitled these two collections 'Hymns,' we can hardly think that most of them were intended to be used in public worship. Their polemic purpose and their contribution to a theological debate was very considerable, but they could not be sung in the Societies, the Bands, the Love Feasts or any other gathering of 'Methodists.' They were too deliberately controversial and provocative to be offered as congregational praise and worship. When John Wesley compiled his definitive edition of hymns in 1779, *A Collection of Hymns for the Use of the People called Methodists*, only a handful of verses from the forty-four hymns that make up these two Collections were included. This was

---

[38] Charles Wesley, *The Poetical Works*, Vol. 3, pp. 35, 36.

not because either John or Charles Wesley had lessened their emphatic emphasis on universal grace. For all time that doctrine was enshrined in hymns that would become universally popular, inside and outside Methodism.

Charles Wesley had spent twenty years in the Bible and had produced thousands of hymns. Now, in the year 1762, he found time to study all the Bible and he used it as a source of many hymns, starting with Genesis and concluding with Revelation. He wrote the *Preface*, saying that he was 'Charles Wesley, M.A., Presbyter of the Church of England.'

> God, having graciously laid His hand upon my body, and disabled me for the principal work of the ministry, has thereby given me an unexpected occasion of writing the following hymns....Several of the hymns are intended to prove, and several to guard, the doctrine of Christian Perfection. I dare not publish one without the other. In the latter sort I use some severity; not against particular persons, but against Enthusiasts and Antinomians, who, by not living up to their profession, give abundant occasion to them that seek it, and cause the truth to be evil spoken of....My desire is, rightly to divide the word of Truth: but who is sufficient for these things? Who can check the self-confident, without discouraging the self-diffident?...Reader, if God ministers grace to thy soul through any of these hymns, give Him the glory, and offer up a prayer for the weak instrument that, whenever I finish my course, I may depart in peace, having seen in Jesus Christ His great salvation.[39]

Between 1739 and 1759, twenty-nine collections of hymns appeared, some bearing the names of John and Charles Wesley and some only having Charles' name. Then in 1762 Charles published two volumes under the title, *Short Hymns on Select Passages of the Holy Scriptures*. In these two volumes Charles systematically wrote verses on all the books of the Bible; from

---

[39] Charles Wesley, *The Poetical Works*, Vol. IX, pp. vii, viii.

Genesis to Malachi, and from Matthew to Revelation. He dealt with all the sixty-six of the biblical canon, including Obadiah, Philemon, 2nd and 3rd John. He produced two volumes of Biblical poetry, running to a total of five thousand, one hundred pieces; one thousand, six hundred and nine pieces based on the Old Testament and three thousand, four hundred and ninety one pieces based on the New Testament. Charles entitled these productions *Short Hymns*. Many of them were just one stanza dealing with the selected scripture passage, while others ran to three, four, five or more stanzas. In all of these five thousand, one hundred poetic pieces, were to stand alone; each of them, whether of one or more stanzas, was complete in itself.

Charles Wesley 'Christianised' the Old Testament. Whether the passage is prophecy or promise, liturgy or law, symbol or sign, parable or precept, command or counsel, poetry or prose, whether spoken by prophet or priest or psalmist – all point forward and all are fulfilled in Christ the Messiah, the Saviour of the world. He set the Old Testament to song and turned many passages from the Pentateuch, the poetical books and the Prophets into lyrical verse. In this way his hymns are a kind of commentary on the Old Testament text. The strength of this commentary is that it makes the text memorable, but the weakness is that in Charles' desire to make every passage speak of Christ and the Christian gospel, the context and the immediate application are mostly ignored.

The surprise we find in Charles Wesley's treatment of the Old Testament is his work on the Psalms. Indeed it often looks as if Charles' outstanding gifts as a lyricist seems to have temporarily deserted him when he worked on the Psalter. And this is all the more surprising because in addition to this systematic treatment of the Psalms, he had also published much better verses in his *Select Psalms*. In general, however, it must be concluded that Charles Wesley was not at his poetic best when he dealt with the Psalms.

In his treatment of the Old Testament, Charles Wesley is never daunted when he meets with names of people and places. With his customary ease he scans them into his text and metre. So we get Adam, Abraham, and Aaron; we get Benjamin, Boaz and Bethlehem; Delila, Sampson and the Philistines; Egyptian and Ethiopian, Gilead, Jonathan, Jerusalem, Jeshurun, Jordan, Jeroboam and Jezabel; Melchisadeck, Pharoah, the Urim and the Thummim – and all the rest as far as Zion and Zerubbabel!

In 1960 the Congregational scholar, Bernard Lord Manning, published his outstanding study, *The Hymns of Wesley and Watts*. In an appreciation of the hymns of Charles Wesley, Manning asked the question: what made Charles so outstandingly good in turning Scripture into powerful and memorable verse?

> There is the full-orbed and conscious orthodoxy of a scholar trained and humbled as he contemplates the holy, catholic and evangelical faith in its historic glory and strength. The hymns are charged with dogma. They set forth …. the peculiar and pungent doctrines of uncompromising Christianity. References to the doctrine of the Holy Trinity, of the Incarnation, of Redemption by the Passion, of the Resurrection – we never move far from these. Simply to state the doctrine of the Holy Trinity is for Wesley a pleasure and a means of grace.[40]

All the great doctrines of 'uncompromising Christianity' are found over and over again in the hymns of Charles Wesley. For half a century, at an average of ten lines every day, of every week, of every month, of every year for fifty years, Charles wrote thousands of hymns that taught the doctrines of God the

---

[40] Bernard Lord Manning, *The Hymns of Wesley and Watts*, 27.

Father, the Son, the Holy Spirit, man, sin, grace, atonement, redemption, regeneration, new birth, justification, witness of the Spirit, sanctification, holiness, the Church, the sacraments, death, judgement, heaven, hell, and the life everlasting.

In fifty years Charles Wesley took a stand against limited atonement, irresistible grace and perseverance. Wherever he found it he made sure that his voice was raised against it and for half a century he was vigorously opposed to it. It was expressed both in his letters and his hymns. In the second issue of their hymns published in 1740, there is a very strong argument that this grace was not given to believers in an instant. John Wesley wrote the *Preface* to this edition and he warned believers not to expect it as already done.

> Neither therefore dare we affirm (as some have done) that this salvation is at once given to true believers. There is indeed an instantaneous (as well as a gradual) work of God in the souls of his children; and their wants not, we know, a cloud of witnesses, who have received in one moment, either a clear sense of the forgiveness of their sins, or the abiding witness of the Holy Spirit. But we do not know a single instance, in any place, of a person's receiving, in one and the same moment, remission of sins, the abiding witness of the Spirit, and a new, a clean heart.... In their trouble they cry unto the Lord, and He shows He hath taken away their sins, and opens the kingdom of heaven in their hearts, even righteousness and peace and joy in the Holy Ghost. Fear and sorrow and pain are fled away and sin hath no more dominion over them.[41]

In the same edition, Charles writes a hymn under the heading, 'After a Relapse into Sin.' We cannot be sure if it was a Christian who fell into sin or if it was Charles himself, but the pain and distress it caused cannot be doubted.

---

[41] John Wesley, *The Poetical Works*, 'The Preface', Vol. 1, pp. 202, 203.

Depth of mercy! Can there be
Mercy still reserved for me?
Can my God His wrath forbear
Me, the chief of sinners, spare?

Whence to *me* this waste of love
Ask my Advocate above
See the cause in Jesu's face
Now before the throne of grace.

If I rightly read Thy heart
If Thou all compassion are
Bow Thine ear, in mercy bow
Pardon and accept me now.[42]

In the same volume of hymns, Charles raises the problem of men and women crying out to God because he never loved them.

Father, whose hand on *all* bestows
Sufficiency of saving grace
Whose universal love o'erflows
The whole of *Adam's* fallen race.

If I could hear Thy quickening call
Then all *may* seek and find Thee too
Surely Thou loving are to all
And I stand forth to prove it true.

But, O, in vain the temper tries
To shake the Rock that ne'er shall move
My steadfast soul His power defies
Secure in this, that God is love.[43]

---

[42] Charles Wesley, *The Poetical Works*, Vol. 1, pp. 271, 272.
[43] Charles Wesley, *The Poetical Works,* Vol. 1, pp. 308, 309.

John and Charles Wesley published another volume of hymns, *Hymns and Sacred Poems*, in 1741. It is called *The Backslider* but we cannot tell whether it is someone close to Wesley or to himself. The two last verses sums it all up.

Let me never, never more
My wretched soul deceive
Dream that I have life, before
I hear Thy voice and live.
Let me, humbled in the dust
Wait to taste how good Thou are
See, and feel, but never trust
My own deceitful heart.

O that I could truly wait
The dictates of Thy will
Calmly mourn my sinful state
Till Thou shalt say, "Be still"
The lost sheep to save I came
The backslider to restore
Sinners I do not condemn
Depart, and sin no more.[44]

Later in the same volume of hymns Charles prayed a prayer of sanctification based on the promises of God.

That I Thy mercy may proclaim
That all mankind Thy truth may see
Hallow Thy great and glorious name
And perfect holiness in me.

---

[44] Charles Wesley, *The Poetical Works*, Vol. 11, pp. 112, 113.

The hatred of the carnal mind
Out of my flesh at once remove
Give me a tender heart, resign'd
And pure, and full of faith and love.

O that I now, from sin released
The word might to the utmost prove
Enter into the promised rest
The *Canaan* of Thy perfect love.[45]

---

[45] Charles Wesley, *The Poetical Works,* Vol. 2, pp. 319, 321.

Epilogue

There are two hymns written by Charles Wesley that deserve a place in every hymn book, especially those published by all who delight in Charles' verse. The first one is called 'Wrestling Jacob.' If John Wesley's comment, in his 1788 Conference obituary note on his brother, can be substantiated, Isaac Watts said of this hymn that it 'was worth all the verses he himself had written.'[46] It also found a place in Arthur Quiller-Couch's, *Oxford Book of English Verse.*[47]

Come, O Thou Traveller unknown
Whom still I hold but cannot see
My company before is gone
And I am left alone with Thee
With Thee all night I mean to stay
And wrestle till the break of day.

Yield to me now, for I am weak
But confident in self-despair
Speak to my heart, in blessings speak
Be conquered by my instant prayer
Speak, or Thou never hence shall move
And tell me if Thy Name is Love.

'Tis Love! 'tis Love, Thou diedst for me
I hear Thy whisper in my heart
The morning breaks, the shadows flee
Pure, Universal love Thou art
To me, to all, Thy mercies move
Thy nature and Thy name is Love.[48]

---

[46] John Wesley, *The Works [BE]*, Vol. 10, p. 646.
[47] Arthur Quiller-Couch, *The Oxford Book of English Verse 1250-1918*, pp. 525, 526.
[48] Charles Wesley, *The Poetical Works*, Vol. 2, pp. 173–176.

Having noted that few verses from the *Hymns on God's Everlasting Love* were included in the 1779 or subsequent editions of Methodist hymns, selected stanzas from one hymn were included. It appeared in all the later editions, up to and including *Hymns and Psalms* (1983), and in nearly all the hymn books published by the various branches of Methodism. By any literary, poetic, or lyrical canon, it stands as one of Charles Wesley's all-time truly great hymns. It expresses so well the evangel that both John and Charles Wesley so successfully disseminated across these kingdoms in the 18th century.

Father, whose *everlasting love*
Thy only Son for sinners gave
Whose grace to *all* did *freely* move
And sent Him down a *world to save*.

Help us Thy mercy to extol
Immense, unfathomed, unconfined
To praise the Lamb who *died for all*
The *general Saviour of Mankind.*

Thy *undistinguishing regard*
Was cast on *Adam's* fallen race
For all Thou hast in Christ prepared
Sufficient, sovereign, saving grace.

A world He suffered to redeem
For *all* He hath the Atonement made
For those that *will not come* to Him
The ransom of His life was paid.

Arise, O God, maintain Thy cause
The fullness of the *Gentiles* call
Lift up the standard of Thy Cross
And *all* shall own Thou diedst for all.[49]

---

[49] Charles Wesley, *The Poetical Works*, Vol. 3, pp. 3-5.

Books by Revd Dr Herbert Boyd McGonigle

William Cooke on Entire Sanctification, Beacon Hill Press, Kansas City, Missouri, 1978.

The Arminianism of John Wesley, Moorleys Print & Publishing, Ilkeston, Derbyshire, 1988.

John Wesley and the Moravians, Moorleys Print & Publishing, Ilkeston, Derbyshire, 1995.

John Wesley's Doctrine of Prevenient Grace, Moorleys Print & Publishing, Ilkeston, Derbyshire, 1995.

Scriptural Holiness: The Wesleyan Distinctive, Moorleys Print & Publishing, Ilkeston, Derbyshire, 1995.

Sufficient Saving Grace: John Wesley's Evangelical Arminianism. 350 pages, Paternoster Publishing, Carlisle, Cumbria, 2001.

To God Be The Glory: The Killadeas Convention 1952-2002, Moorleys Print & Publishing, Ilkeston, Derbyshire, 2002.

John Wesley's Arminian Theology: An Introduction. Moorleys Print & Publishing, Ilkeston, Derbyshire, 2005.

A Burning and a Shining Light: The Life and Ministry of William Bramwell. Moorleys Print & Publishing, Ilkeston, Derbyshire, 2009.

Christianity or Deism? John Wesley's Response to John Taylor's Denial of the Doctrine of Original Sin. Moorleys Print & Publishing, Ilkeston, Derbyshire, 2012.

John Wesley: Exemplar of the Catholic Spirit. Moorleys Print & Publishing , Ilkeston, Derbyshire, 2014.